REFERENCE -- NOT TO BE
TAKEN FROM THIS ROOM

Ref.
720.228
Bus

LIBRARY

W9-DFN-491

THE ART OF THE
ARCHITECTURAL
MODEL

AKIKO BUSCH

DESIGN PRESS

To Noel and Lucian Johnston

First Edition, First Printing

Copyright (c) 1991 by Akiko Busch

Printed in Hong Kong

Designed by Ann Gold

Reproduction or republication of the content in any manner, without the
express written permission of the publisher, is prohibited.
The publisher takes no responsibility for the use of any of the materials
or methods described in this book, or for the products thereof.
Library of Congress Cataloging-in-Publication Data

Busch, Akiko
The art of the architectural model / Akiko Busch.
p.   cm.
Includes bibliographical references.
ISBN 0-8306-9969-4
1. Architectural models.   I. Title.
NA2790.B87   1990
720'.228—dc20   90-3245
CIP

Design Press offers posters and The Cropper, a device for cropping artwork,
for sale. For information, contact Mail-order Department.
Design Press books are available at special discounts for bulk purchases
for sales promotions, fund raisers, or premiums. For details contact
Special Sales Manager. Questions regarding the content of the book
should be addressed to:

Design Press
11 West 19th Street
New York, NY 10010

Design Press book are published by Design Press, an imprint of
TAB BOOKS. TAB BOOKS is a Division of McGraw-Hill, Inc. The
Design Press logo is a trademark of TAB BOOKS.

PAGE 1
Proposed Times Square Center, New York, New York.
Architect: John Burgee Architects; formerly Johnson/Burgee Architects.
Model builder: Awad Architectural Models. Photographer: © Nathaniel Lieberman

PAGE 2
580 California Street, San Francisco, California. Architect: John Burgee Architects;
formerly Johnson/Burgee Architects. Model builder: Ron Marian, Joe Chun, Rob Berryman
Photographer: © Bob Harr, Hedrich-Blessing

ACKNOWLEDGMENTS

For sharing their wealth of information with me in the preparation of this book, I am most indebted to the model builders themselves. While all those who shared their expertise with me are too numerous to mention here, I am especially grateful to Theodore Conrad; George Awad at Awad Architectural Models; Elaine O'Sullivan at Scale Models Unlimited; Leslie Oberlander at 3-D Design; Harold Gilstein at Skidmore, Owings & Merrill; and Eugene Cervini at Scale Images, Inc.

Of enormous help too were the photographers, and their agents, who generously contributed to this book, most specifically: Steve Rosenthal; Erica Stoller at ESTO; Michael O. Houlahan at Hedrich-Blessing; and Jim Steinkemp at Steinkemp/Ballogg.

My thanks as well to Marc Miller at the Queens Museum; Joanne Lehrfeld at Robert A. M. Stern Architects; Janet Adams at I. M. Pei & Partners; and Nancy Cheung at Kohn Pedersen Fox Associates PC.

C O N T E N T S

THE ART OF THE
ARCHITECTURAL MODEL

INTRODUCTION

Archaeologists studying pre-Hispanic culture in Mexico have observed that the Indians did not use the wheel for any practical purpose of their own until the Spaniards introduced the wheeled cart as a means of transportation. The curious twist to the story is that among these civilizations many small wheeled toys and animal figures dating back to the first millennium have been found.

While what we want or aspire to may often be larger than life, what is smaller than life is generally more easily negotiated. Our enchantment with the miniature is rooted in the sense of power it instills in us. The world in miniature grants us a sense of authority; it is more easily maneuvered and manipulated, more easily observed and understood. Moreover, when we fabricate, touch, or simply observe the miniature, we have entered into a private affair; the sense of closeness, of intimacy is implicit. Whether it is something as concrete and useful as a wheel or a more abstract and subtle truth, the discoveries we make through models can have a value of much greater proportions.

As a controlled environment, models appeal to the builder in all of us, at all ages. As children we develop our notions of the environment—and our place in it—through miniatures. Dollhouses, barnyards, fortresses, battlegrounds, and complex railway systems are the dwarf landscapes upon which we act out our childhood discoveries and revelations. Such miniature habitats serve a more clinical role too and indeed are frequently used by child psychologists in analyzing the child's view of social interactions. A dollhouse, for example, and the events the child stages therein may reveal much about his feelings toward the way his family interacts.

Models have a place in our adult life as well. For the Japanese the landscape of the miniature expresses a more spiritual sense of placement. The arrangement of rocks and sand and perhaps a single shrub in traditional Japanese stone gardens may evoke a panorama of mountains, valleys, rivers, and oceans. Such condensing of the natural world is not meant simply to represent or re-create nature but to symbolize the spiritual enlightenment one might find there. The fantastic shapes and forms

Vertical Complex. Lynne Clibanoff, 1987. Masonite, plywood, and acrylic construction with electric light. Courtesy of HIMONT Incorporated.

1 1

found in many of these stone gardens resonate with symbolism and reflect a profound animism in which immutable stones are endowed with spiritual power.

Similarly, miniature Persian and Indian paintings are a microcosm of the splendors, horrors, and erotica of religious myths, folk legends, and court life. But it is the scale of the paintings that gives these stories their intimacy. Indeed, the viewer marvels all the more at the epic nature of these narratives when they are conveyed through such condensed, articulate images and frames.

In more recent years, numerous artists and sculptors have chosen variations on model making as a means of more social discourse. There is an atmosphere that is at once beguiling and intimate about the model, and artists who choose this format seem almost to propose a private dialogue with the viewer. Artist Laura Foreman has constructed a series of birdhouses as metaphorical expressions, explaining that "the bird-house metaphor stands as a personal metaphor of contradiction: the desire to be totally free and unencumbered and the need to be totally secure and protected." Foreman's symbolic dwellings represent possibilities of natural resting places in the artificial urban terrain.

Lynne Clibanoff's miniature interiors, though encapsulated in boxes that can be measured in inches, allude to greater, more mysterious, and often more ominous dimensions. Receding corridors, tunnels, and archways illuminated by unexpected light sources create a sense of spaciousness that is at once sinister and dreamlike. Despite being well lit, there is something obscure about these model rooms. That these dimensions are played out on such a confined stage is, of course, what makes them provocative.

Ceramic artist Tim Prythero constructs perfect miniature trailer parks. His pieces precisely transcribe the clutter, the debris, the general dilapidation, and ironically, the stationary condition of these houses on wheels. Cinder blocks, old tires, torn screen doors, faded awnings, and stained aluminum siding have all been replicated in perfect scale in this downsizing of two of the more popular American dreams—owning one's own home and moving west, moving on.

Artist Michael McMillen conveys a different sense of history in his pieces. His precarious constructs suggest that time, and the decay that inevitably accompanies it, is a vertical progression. In *Astoria* one dilapidated shed is perched on another, and that on another, their tin sides rusting and their wood rotting, as though there were some organic growth to the sense of abandonment. In *Generator* rotting walls and floorboards seem almost to bloom on an even more frail skeletal structure.

Sculptor Charles Simonds takes a different direction in his miniatures of the impermanent. His undersize buildings and villages, composed of minute unfired clay "bricks," are models of decay rather than construction. Poised on vacant windowsills, doorways, and curbs, their demise was inevitable. Scattered across New York City's Lower East Side like miniature archaeological sites, these pieces document urban decay rather than the splendors of urban architecture celebrated by most architectural models.

The language of architecture has been picked up by product designers in more whimsical expressions. Consider the spirals of Frank Lloyd Wright's Guggenheim Museum reproduced as an eggcup or Boston's John Hancock Center as a floor lamp or Le Corbusier's Ronchamp as a cigarette box. All of these irreverent reproductions of architectural icons of the modern age are the work of Italian architect Alberto Vaccarone. And furniture maker Duane Huntington has fashioned seating from the forms of the Transamerica pyramid, the twin towers of the World Trade Center, and the Chippendale roofline of New York's AT&T building. The charm of these pieces lies in their incongruity; there is something innately appealing, albeit ridiculous, in asking such imposing urban landmarks to perform lesser, more mundane tasks.

While it is not unreasonable to expect artists, sculptors, and furniture designers to be drawn to the language of architecture, it is more startling to find vernacular inspiring bakers—as indeed it did in the series of models designed for "Edible Architecture, Delicious Designs," an exhibit and subsequent benefit auction sponsored by Steelcase Design Partnership in the fall of 1989. Gingerbread is, after all, more familiar to architects as a metaphor than as a material, and it was the purpose of the exhibit to correct this. The exhibit took to a new and fantastic extreme the conventional truth that the technological age presents architects with the constant challenge of working with new materials: the models were constructed not in the vinyl, acrylic, and foamcore more familiar to architects, but in pastry, butter cream, spun sugar, chocolate, gingerbread, and even Chiclets. Here, in constructs sure to sweeten the disposition of even the most irascible client, the model was the format for an unlikely collaboration between architects and bakers.

The language of architecture, and miniaturization in particular, has been picked up by artists in a variety of other media. Architectural models are a common format for social and aesthetic discourses. In introducing the exhibit "Miniature Environments" shown at the Whitney Museum of American Art at Philip Morris, Josephine Gear wrote, "The miniaturization of scale is a strategy for making art unintimidating and approachable and for inducing physical—and emotional—proximity. The affective nature of miniature artworks comes from childhood associations, which the toylike scale activates, and from the sense of secretiveness or of sharing private visions that smallness engenders."

It might follow, then, that architectural models, *as used by architects*, similarly induce a more intellectual proximity. While the models constructed and used by architects have an altogether different set of concerns and may seem to have little in common with these other miniatures, they nevertheless are the most efficient way to translate ideas, a way of collecting and articulating the precise spatial information about a proposed building. If architecture is ultimately and inevitably a public statement, then the architectural model is a preliminary and more intimate dialogue with the facts of building.

Study models built by architects are more than three-dimensional renderings of elevation drawings. They are ways of testing proportion and scale, determining schematic massing, examining the relationship of horizontal and vertical planes that will eventually define the interior and exterior of the building.

Finished models and presentation models provide a way of presenting this information to the client, a way of making the spatial facts of the architecture accessible to those outside of the profession. In recent years the use of such presentation models has grown significantly. No longer are they simply elaborate constructions to present to the client. Rather, in urban areas, they are often crucial to the approval of development applications. Presented to local community and planning boards and zoning committees, such models may be used to demonstrate the proposed building's relation to its site, its effect on traffic patterns, its visual connection to surrounding architecture, its scale to neighboring buildings, and its overall impact on the neighborhood.

Finally, the role served by the model does not end with the proposed building's approval. Increasingly, presentation models are used to sell space in the proposed building, and the contemporary architectural model is a marketing tool as much as it is a design tool. With urban real estate commanding the high prices that it does, a model that leases a single floor even a month earlier has just paid for itself.

With models playing such a critical role in the design and planning process, it comes as no surprise that the art and the industry of model making has become increasingly sophisticated in recent years. The array of modern synthetic materials and technology available to the model maker has yielded new standards of precision and speed. With the use of laser technology especially, models can be rapidly assembled to represent not simply the form of the proposed building but the minute details of its facade finishes and textures too. In some cases the cost of such models can reach five or six hundred thousand dollars, an expense that nevertheless remains easily justified by anticipated revenues to the building's developer.

With the increased use of costly and sophisticated equipment in model shops, many in-house shops and studios within architectural firms have been disbanded. Rather than purchase the costly equipment and expand the capabilities of their own in-house shops, most architectural firms have found it more cost-effective to contract out for the construction of their presentation models. While architects may continue to construct their own study models from foamcore or illustration board, the more precise and polished presentation models are constructed by better-equipped shops independent of the architectural firm. And as this increasingly becomes the case, the construction of architectural models is no longer a sideline to the architectural profession, but an industry unto itself, an art demanding its own skill and vision.

As a device that critically influences the final shape of our built environment, the architectural model has a value that far exceeds its miniature scale. Yet the art and the craft that go into model construction are often overlooked for obvious reasons. These models are constructed for temporary use. Because the architectural firms or developers that have commissioned them rarely have the storage space or the incentive to keep them, models are frequently dismantled or destroyed after they have served their purpose. They are not made for permanence. So not only is the territory of the architectural model on a diminutive scale, so too is the time it inhabits. Models take up little space and brief time, factors that together intensify their message all the more.

In addition, architectural models are supportive devices. Because they are built to represent a larger art—that of the building itself—the craftsmanship and skill that have gone into their construction can be easily overlooked.

It is the purpose of this book, then, not to elevate the model to a status greater than it deserves but to examine and illustrate its own small but significant splendors; to celebrate the surface and structure of that diminutive landscape upon which so many of our larger, life-size endeavors are later carried out.

LEFT

Generator. Michael C. McMillen, 1987 – 88. Painted wood and metal construction. Collection of William Dreyfuss. Courtesy of Patricia Hamilton Gallery, New York, New York.

ABOVE

Astoria. Michael C. McMillen, 1987. Painted wood and metal construction. Collection of Helene Wasserman. Courtesy of Patricia Hamilton Gallery, New York, New York.

Rietveld House. Private
Collection, New York; Courtesy
of Barry Friedman Ltd., New
York, New York.

TOP

Classic Cake. Robert A. M.
Stern, architect; Colette Peters,
baker. Edible materials. Courtesy
of The Steelcase Design
Partnership. Photograph ©
Elliott Kaufman, New York.

LEFT

Edible Parthenon. Deborah
Sussman and Debra Valencia,
Sussman/Prejza & Company,
designers; Rosemary Littman,
baker. Edible materials. Courtesy
of The Steelcase Design
Partnership. Photograph ©
Elliott Kaufman, New York.

ABOVE

The Wedding. Lynne Clibanoff, 1985. Masonite, plywood, and acrylic construction with electric light.

RIGHT

Untitled. Lynne Clibanoff, 1988. Masonite, plywood, and acrylic construction with electric light.

Rocks III. Charles Simonds,
1984. Unfired clay. © Charles
Simonds. Courtesy of Leo
Castelli Gallery, New York,
New York.

TOP

Shell Premium and Regular. Tim
Prythero, 1985. Mixed media.
Courtesy of Craig Cornelius
Gallery, New York, New York.

BOTTOM

O.K. Service. Tim Prythero,
1986. Mixed media. Collection of
Fran and Howard Schoor.
Courtesy of Craig Cornelius
Gallery, New York, New York.

TOP

Trailer with Bottle Fence and Cactus Planters. Tim Prythero, 1983. Mixed media. Courtesy of Craig Cornelius Gallery, New York, New York.

LEFT

Battleship Trailer. Tim Prythero, 1984. Mixed media. Courtesy of Craig Cornelius Gallery, New York, New York.

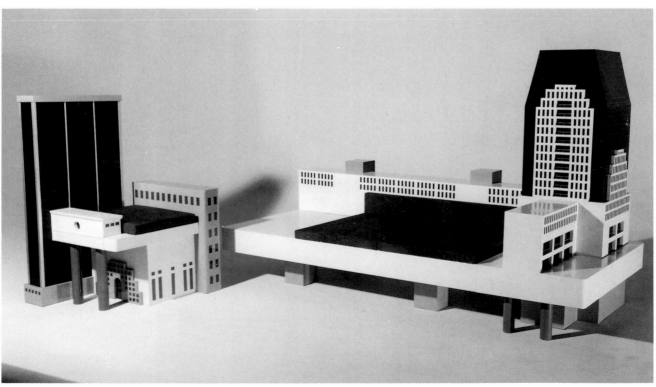

OPPOSITE
Assorted furniture. Duane Huntington, 1987 – 88. Painted birch veneer plywood.

ABOVE
People's Peepshow Birdhouse. Laura Foreman, 1989. Mixed media. Courtesy of Souyun Yi Gallery, New York, New York.

LEFT
Birdhouse. Laura Foreman, 1989. Mixed media, including cassette player and headphones with tape loop with selections by Charlie Parker including ''Ornithology.'' Courtesy of Souyun Yi Gallery, New York, New York.

THE POWER OF
THE MODEL:

ARCHITECTURE IN AND OUT OF CONTEXT

In recent years architecture, and urban architecture especially, has been challenged by a new set of standards. The technological and engineering extravaganzas exemplified in urban office towers of previous decades have been replaced by a new set of concerns, such as the building's recognition of its site, including landscape, adjacent buildings and streets; its historic context; its energy efficiency; and its overall compatibility with the existing environment. Services and amenities became the keynotes of urban building. And while some office towers do continue to be constructed as monuments to a single corporate presence—with the ego of the architect nearly as dominant—the most innovative and progressive urban building recognizes that it is a part of a larger environment and makes some effort to meld with it. This can be in the form of urban office towers that serve as retail shopping plazas with restaurants and parking or in mixed-used commercial buildings that are integrated in downtown areas alongside more recreational and civic buildings. Or it can simply be in a design that is less intent on structural and visual theatrics and more on developing a restrained and integrated, even background, building style.

Likewise, corporate office parks in the suburbs are inclined to search out a more organic fusion with their landscape. Recognition of environmental concerns boosts corporate public image. Too, such awareness as expressed in articulate landscaping with walkways, waterways, and shade trees can work to soften what might otherwise be perceived as an aggressive corporate presence.

The form these new buildings take reflects the change in attitude. Less linear than the architecture of previous decades, they are more layered and textured, more decorative and more attentive to color. Atrium buildings have almost become a symbol of this new building type. The covered and light-filled interior courtyard promotes a festive atmosphere and in general seems to encourage a human exchange that the more austere architecture of previous decades tended to neglect.

If these are some of the new concerns of contemporary architecture, the presentation model can be instrumental in determining how successfully a proposed building

Mellon Bank Center,
Philadelphia, Pennsylvania
Architect: Kohn Pedersen Fox
Associates PC
Model builder: Awad Architectural
Models

will satisfy them. Two sets of models constructed for the ongoing Times Square Redevelopment Project in New York City reflect to what degree "context" has become an issue in urban building. Currently an urban midway featuring adult bookstores, peep shows, drug dealers, and a decidedly criminal element alongside legitimate movie theaters, the theater district, a festival of electronic billboards, and restaurants, Times Square is ripe for redevelopment. The nature of the redevelopment plan, which includes the construction of office towers and the renovation of numerous theaters, has been the center of controversy for nearly a decade. An early model illustrates a plan for a group of office towers that would have lent a solid and dignified presence to the area. Historical details such as mansard roofs replete with turrets are whimsical, but for the most part, the buildings are elegant, somber, serious.

Critics charged, however, that the serious and somber design of the buildings was not consistent with the more festive mood of Times Square, and a model submitted in 1989 reflects the changes inspired by these allegations. Mansard rooflines have been angled, bands of color inserted, and facades seem to have been punched, incised, and bent into different shapes. More to the point, however, is the electronic signage—in keeping with the glittering neon of the Great White Way—that has been incorporated into the architecture. Whether the revised design is more than a stylistic revision is still open to question, but the model clearly indicates at least some recognition of urban context.

Likewise, models for the addition to Frank Lloyd Wright's Guggenheim Museum illustrate the original design and two subsequent revisions. As a senior associate on the project remarked, the plan went from "an objectlike approach to a background approach." Opposition to the addition, voiced by a loose affiliation of community groups and local historic groups, was centered on the architectural blasphemy of altering a Frank Lloyd Wright masterpiece. More specifically, objections included the scale of the addition as well as the argument that the new building would cause occupants of neighboring buildings to lose their views of Central Park. In response, the architects refined the original design, reducing the height and eliminating approximately five thousand square feet.

While architectural models of individual buildings can work as miniature test zones for urban awareness and responsibility and can indeed be used as effective tools in urban planning, a more grand device is a model of the city itself. The most notable example of such is the Panorama of New York City, on view at the Queens Museum. Robert Moses conceived the idea and hired the firm of Raymond Lester Associates to construct the expansive model. Using aerial photographs, street maps, and photographs of individual buildings, the model makers worked on a scale of one inch to one hundred feet and reduced the city limits to about nine thousand square feet, nevertheless complete with some 835,000 buildings.

Moses saw the model, constructed for the 1964 – 65 World's Fair, not simply as a temporary public exhibit but as a precise, permanent, and utilitarian planning tool. As planner and architect for city parks, housing projects, expressways, and bridges, indeed the major arteries leading to and from the city, Moses considered the model, representing the five boroughs in minute detail, to be an ongoing resource for "architectural firms, community groups, city agencies and others involved in the growth and management of New York City." The Panorama serves as an educational tool for school children as well. A lighting system indicating schools, hospitals, police and fire headquarters, museums, and other city facilities familiarizes children with the vast network of city resources.

Other city models attempt even more. In the Environmental Research Laboratory in Berkeley, California, a model of the city of San Francisco attempts to record climate both by re-creating patterns of sunlight and shadow and by measuring the erratic wind patterns of that hilly coastal city. But while the intent and scope of such models may indeed be broad, there are limits to what even they can achieve. The Panorama cannot represent time—or the building boom that has occurred in New York City over time. Indeed, with only sporadic updating, the Panorama today represents New York partially as it was then, partially as it is now: while the twin towers of the World Trade Center have been added to its miniature skyline, there is neither a South Street Seaport nor a Jacob Javits Convention Center, and the model represents the metropolis stilled in a twilight zone of time.

Architecture, more than any other art, is subject to the passage of time. As in the other arts, styles of expression change, and so with them do our perceptions. How we perceive a beaux arts building today is quite different from how it was perceived in 1880. But more to the point is that buildings suffer over time; they age and decay, crumbling visibly and dramatically before our eyes. Moreover, the landscape surrounding a building changes constantly, and adjacent buildings can represent an array of varying architectural periods and styles. All of these inevitably affect the way we perceive a single building. Time is an inescapable condition of architecture.

And architectural models, however precise and finely tooled, are incapable of representing this condition. While their value as study, presentation, and planning tools may be immense, it is also limited.

In viewing architectural models, whether a model of a single building or an entire city, it is important to bear in mind such limitations. In the model world, buildings are stilled, pristine. They bear no vestiges of time and weather. They are untouched by the gritty substances of urban life. Nor are they able to convey the less tangible, atmospheric qualities of architecture—how it feels to stand inside a sprawling stadium or feel the light flooding through a south-facing glazed wall. All of which is to say, it is in the nature of models to remove architecture from its context.

In writing about architectural models in a 1988 issue of *American Craft* magazine, Jeremy Lebensohn observed, "As a sales and promotional tool for developers, architects, and urban planners, models represent projects in their idealized state, often in a manipulated context or out of context altogether. The model offers us a Gulliver's view of a Lilliputian world, its seduction of scale reinforcing the sense of our powers to control the environment, whether it be unbroken countryside, a city block or the interior of a room. Tied by an umbilical cord to the architectural and engineering professions, model making enjoys a symbiotic relationship to both without being absorbed or losing its identity as a separate but allied art."

This, then, is the underlying irony that viewers might keep in mind when examining models. The models shown on the following pages illustrate the enormous range, diversity, and complexity of contemporary architectural models. In surface, structure, design, and engineering, these models are increasingly sophisticated building extravaganzas in their own right. And with their new-age exactitude, they are capable of representing the proposed building—its scale and massing, its materials, its lighting, its decorative finishes and flourishes—with unfailing precision. Nevertheless, these models inevitably idealize their subjects. They represent architecture in a perfect world. By their very nature, they remove buildings from their context. And context is all the more important to contemporary architecture.

That architectural models make an effort to delineate the building precisely *and* to represent it in a pure, ideal state is the irony and the incongruity of contemporary model making. It is the factor to keep foremost in mind when viewing the models shown on these pages. But there can be magic in incongruity and a greater intelligence drawn from absorbing two seemingly contradictory ideas at once. This duality in the nature of model making does not necessarily lessen the value of the model. Rather, this paradox gives them their beauty and complexity, ultimately bestowing upon models their own singular identity.

The Panorama, New York,
New York
Model builder: Raymond Lester
and Associates
Photographer: © Dan
Cornish/ESTO

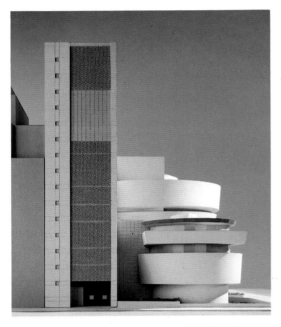

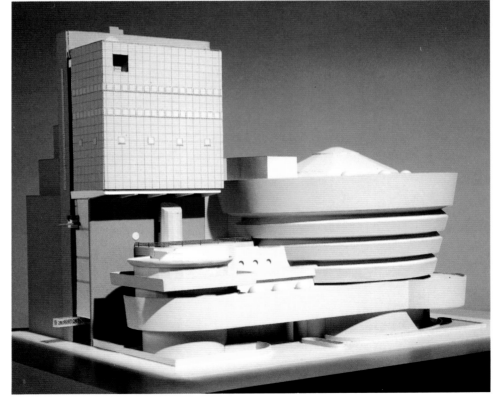

Proposed addition to the
Solomon R. Guggenheim
Museum, New York, New York
At right is the earliest model.
The two photographs above
show the second model;
opposite is the final model.
Architect: Gwathmey Siegel &
Associates
Model builder: Scale Images, Inc.
Photographer: © Dan
Cornish/ESTO

Proposed Times Square Center,
New York, New York
Above is the first model; at left,
the second.
Architect: John Burgee
Architects; formerly
Johnson/Burgee Architects
Model builder: Awad Architectural
Models
Photographer: © Nathaniel
Lieberman

Canal + Headquarters,
Paris, France
Architect: Richard Meier &
Partners Architects
Model builder: Scale Images, Inc.
Photographer: Ezra Stoller
© ESTO

3 4

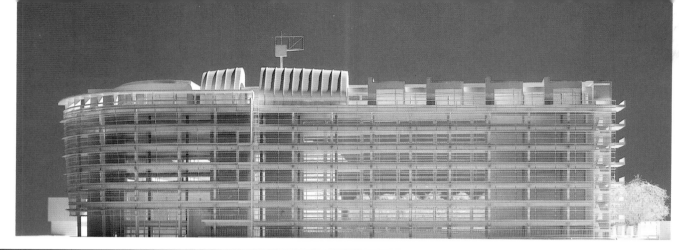

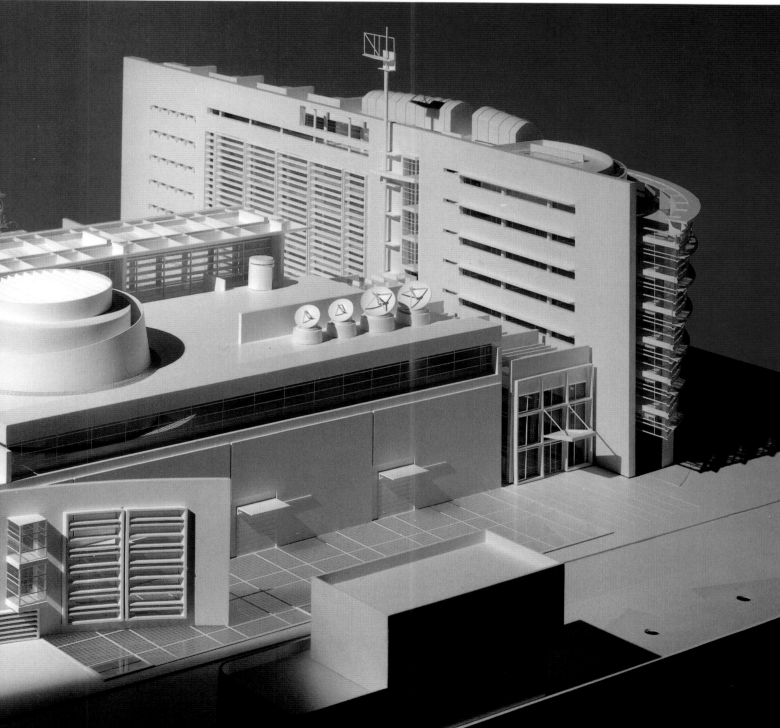

ABOVE

Park Center, Calgary, Canada

Architect: Kohn Pedersen Fox

Associates PC

Model builder: Awad Architectural

Models

RIGHT

Hercules Incorporated

Headquarters, Wilmington,

Delaware

Architect: Kohn Pedersen Fox

Associates PC

Model builder: Awad Architectural

Models

101 Federal Street, Boston, Massachusetts
Architect: Kohn Pedersen Fox Associates PC
Model builder: Awad Architectural Models
Photographer: © Jock Pottle/ESTO

OPPOSITE

First Bank Place, Minneapolis, Minnesota
Architect: I. M. Pei & Partners
Model builder: Gabriel Models
Photographer: © Nathaniel Lieberman

LEFT

1250 Boulevard Rene-Levesque, Montreal, Canada
Architect: Kohn Pedersen Fox Associates PC
Model builder: Awad Architectural Models
Photographer: © Jock Pottle/ESTO

TOP
Mainzer Landstrasse 58,
Frankfurt am Main,
West Germany
Architect: Kohn Pedersen Fox
Associates PC
Model builder: Awad Architectural
Models
Photographer: © Jock
Pottle/ESTO

RIGHT AND OPPOSITE
Jacob K. Javits Convention
Center, New York, New York
Architect: I. M. Pei & Partners
Model builder: I. M. Pei &
Partners
Photographer: © Nathaniel
Lieberman

ABOVE AND RIGHT
Grand Harbor, Vero Beach,
Florida
Architect: Robert A. M. Stern
Architects
Model builder: Robert A. M.
Stern Architects

OPPOSITE
International Headquarters, Mexx
International, B.V., Voorschoten,
Netherlands
Architect: Robert A. M. Stern
Architects
Model builder: Robert A. M.
Stern Architects

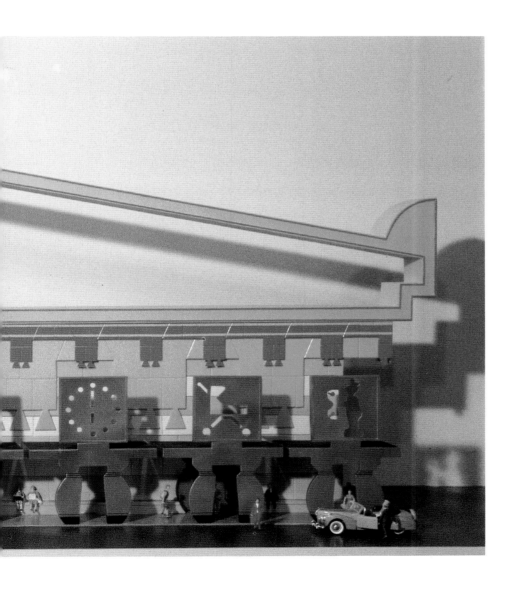

Best Products Catalog
Showroom
Architect: Robert A. M. Stern
Architects
Model builder: Robert A. M.
Stern Architects

OPPOSITE

Mid America Plaza,
Oak Brook, Illinois
Architect: Shaw and Associates
Model builder: The Model Studio
Photographer: Bob Harr,
Hedrich-Blessing

LEFT

123 North Wacker Drive,
Chicago, Illinois
Architect: Perkins & Will
Model builder: Richard Rush
Photographer: Bob Shimer,
Hedrich-Blessing

ABOVE

Market Tower, Indianapolis,
Indiana
Architect: Lohan Associates
Model builder: Syed Ahmed,
Lohan Associates
Photographer: Bob Shimer,
Hedrich-Blessing

OPPOSITE
Southeast Financial Center,
Miami, Florida
Architect: Skidmore, Owings &
Merrill
Model builder: David H. Gibson
Company
Photographer: Bob Harr,
Hedrich-Blessing

LEFT
The NBC Tower at Cityfront
Center, Chicago, Illinois
Architect: Skidmore, Owings &
Merrill
Model builder: Skidmore, Owings
& Merrill/Chicago Model Shop
Photographer: Nick Merrick,
Hedrich-Blessing

TOP

Manufacturers Hanover Plaza,
Wilmington, Delaware
Architect: Skidmore, Owings &
Merrill
Model builder: Skidmore, Owings
& Merrill Model Shop
Photographer: Bob Harr,
Hedrich-Blessing

RIGHT

Harold Washington Library,
Chicago, Illinois
Architect: Skidmore, Owings &
Merrill
Model builder: Scale Models
Unlimited
Photographer: © Nick Merrick,
Hedrich-Blessing

190 LaSalle, Chicago, Illinois
Architect: John Burgee
Architects; formerly
Johnson/Burgee Architects
Model builder: Scale Images, Inc.
Photographer: Bob Harr,
Hedrich-Blessing

ABOVE

RepublicBank Tower,
Dallas, Texas
Architect: Skidmore, Owings &
Merrill
Model builder: The Model Shop,
Scott Harrington
Photographer: Bob Harr,
Hedrich-Blessing

RIGHT

Leo Burnett Company
Headquarters, Chicago, Illinois
Architect: Kevin Roche John
Dinkeloo and Associates
Model builder: Robert M. Hurwit
& Associates
Photographer: Bob Harr,
Hedrich-Blessing

101 California Street, San
Francisco, California
Architect: John Burgee
Architects with Philip Johnson
Model builder: David H. Gibson
Company
Photographer: Bob Harr,
Hedrich-Blessing

MATERIALS OF
THE MINIATURE

I n the last forty years, the craft of building architectural models has become increasingly complex and sophisticated. Standards of precision and detail have been raised significantly, and presentation models are often extraordinarily authentic, albeit minute, representations of the real thing. A 1958 article in *Architectural Forum* noted, "The new models, miniatures though they are, can hardly be considered simply imitations of buildings. They *are* buildings, with their own complex engineering and construction problems." The article went on to note that among the factors for this revolution in the craft was the increased demand on the part of "architects and their clients for exceedingly realistic and accurate model design studies"—demands that are made more urgently today, thirty years later, by developers and their marketing departments.

The revolution in the craft also reflects the changes that architecture itself has undergone. The austere planes of International-style architecture of the Modern period demanded comparatively less detail work on the part of the model maker. Modular units, exposed steel skeletal structures, clean masonry planes, and ribbon windows could be reproduced in miniature relatively easily. Contemporary architecture, however, has reacted vigorously to such simplicity with an onslaught of historical detailing, more colorful materials, and texture combinations. Decoration is no longer taboo. Five different stones or marbles may be specified for the exterior of a single building; masonry, metal, and woods of varying color and grain may all articulate a single facade. Multiple layers, colors, and materials are the vocabulary of contemporary building, and transcribing this multiplicity has likewise transfigured the craft of model making.

But if the buildings—and their models—have become more visually complex, more layered, more detailed, and more decorated, the tools and the materials the model maker uses to achieve this diversity have kept pace. The paper, wood, and plaster of paris that were the tools of the model maker at the beginning of this century continue to be used by some studios, although those model makers who choose to

75 Federal Street, Boston, Massachusetts
Architect: Kohn Pedersen Fox Associates PC
Model builder: Awad Architectural Models
Materials: Plexiglas and vinyl

work with traditional materials tend to rely on more contemporary illustration boards and foamcore as well. While such materials are frail, they are easy to work by hand and are particularly suited to design and study models, where the use of power tools is not cost-effective. More often, though, Plexiglas, vinyl, and acrylics tend to replace these traditional materials.

While some studios prepare presentation models almost exclusively in traditional wood, paper, and illustration board, they are also equipped with table saws, band saws, sanders, joiners, and drill presses. Despite the availability of more durable plastics, these model makers have found that stiff papers and wood have an inherent warmth and texture lacking in synthetic materials. Paper models convey an innate flexibility; they are by nature less imposing than plastic models, and such flexibility, even in presentation models, can be appealing to clients.

Paper construction also tends to be quicker than building with Plexiglas, which requires precise sanding, joining, and painting. A less forgiving material, Plexiglas demands more technical coordination. Paper models, on the other hand, can be revised more easily, and the mat knife can do in an hour what might take a day with plastics. Despite the hopes and intentions of the architect, even presentation models often undergo series of revisions after they have been presented to the client, and the flexibility of working in paper and the subsequent cost benefits are obvious advantages.

Photographic techniques are used by model makers as well, and not simply by those who are already inclined to work in paper. A marble facade, for example, can be represented by a photograph of a real marble slab that is then reduced and reprinted on paper with an adhesive backing that can be attached to the model. Likewise, in interior models a carpet with a texture that is especially difficult to reproduce or a wallpaper with distinctive patterning might best be represented through photography.

Drawbacks to working in paper are, of course, its fragility and its inability to stand up over time. In addition, the finishes the architect specifies for the building must be specified to the model maker before construction. For a plastic model that is to be airbrushed after construction, such specifications can be made after the model has been built, giving the architect the often necessary extra time to determine finishes with the client. Paper models, however, take paint poorly—the edges of cardboard absorb paint differently than the sides do, and the overall surface tends to look fuzzy. Because paper models therefore must be constructed with a paper that accurately represents the color and texture of the building's finish, the exterior finish must be specified by the architect before model construction begins. Finally, the flammability factor is a disadvantage in a model that is to accommodate electricity, even with the use of a plastic lightbox. Despite these drawbacks, however, a number of model makers continue to work largely in paper for the speed, flexibility, and cost-efficiency that the material allows.

Wood appeals to model makers for some of the same reasons—warmth, personality, softness that synthetics lack. Among the woods used most frequently are: cherry, a durable hardwood that can still be easily shaped and which is valued for its warm reddish tones and tendency to bleach light naturally; walnut, valued for its distinctive grain patterns and dark hues; and mahogany, valued for its tight grain. A model for the "Campanile" lighthouse designed by Helpern Architects and constructed of alternating bands of blond basswood and cherry with darker walnut rooftops exploits the visual effect of contrasting tones and grains of different woods.

A model of a large Shingle-style residence illustrates the warmth and flexibility of wood. With the exception of the Plexiglas used for window panels, the entire model was constructed with basswood, which was then painted with watercolors. The surface materials represented include the building's granite base, cedar shingles, a graduated slate roof, and clay chimney pots.

The danger of working with wood, however, is that the model may become simply a picturesque study of wood grains. That is, unless the scale of the model is small and the grain of the wood tight, the model may better demonstrate the texture and grain of wood than it does the architectural design. Such grain patterning can work to an advantage, however, when the model illustrates the schematic massing of a group of buildings, such as the model constructed for the MTA West Side Yards. Because such models are not intended to represent fine architectural detailing or even fenestration, wood grains evince their own detail and warmth. The same model constructed in Plexiglas is likely to be more monotonous.

The use of wood can also be particularly apt in conjunction with other materials. A wood veneer box with the appropriate cutouts can be fitted over a Plexiglas box to make a dramatic rendering of a building with a great deal of fenestration. Or, as in the models of the Commonwealth Center and Shearson Lehman Hutton buildings, details from elevation drawings can be cut and glued to a wood model for study models.

Despite the continued use of paper, illustration board, and wood in many model shops, the advent of vinyl, Lucite, Plexiglas, and aluminum have radically altered the surface and structure of most presentation models. Besides being obviously suited for models of buildings with glass facades, transparent acrylics such as Plexiglas also have the advantages of being durable and lightweight, more flexible than wood, and easier to fabricate. Vinyl, on the other hand, has a more consistent thickness and can be scored more reliably to simulate different textures. Both can be glued in seconds and are less vulnerable than paper and wood to fluctuations in temperature and humidity; they do not shrink, are easily machined, and leave a clean finish.

Milling machines, lathes, saws, and paint sprayers have also become standard tools of the model maker. Milling machines used in model shops, a variation of the standard model, have a fixed motor connected to a table beneath. The table can move in two different directions, permitting three-dimensional pieces to be carved quickly and precisely. The applications of milling machines are obvious when one considers the necessity in model building of reproducing many identical units, ranging from skylights and gables to pieces of furniture.

The tool that perhaps has most changed the model maker's trade is the laser cutter. Capable of cutting sections of plastic, fiberglass, wood, cardboard, paper, and cloth to $1/1000$ of an inch, laser cutters permit precision work in a fraction of the time required previously. When used in conjunction with a CAD system, blueprints can be translated into three dimensions even more efficiently: drawings made on a CAD file can be transferred directly to the computer-driven laser system, reducing costly labor.

The applications of the laser cutter are extensive, from elaborate fenestration cutouts and mullion details to complex trusswork and surface patterning of stone, brick, and other paving materials. And because architectural models are usually constructed in a series of layers, the delicate cutting and scoring abilities of the laser have permitted a new standard of detail. Previously such details may have been represented by hand drawing or painting. However precise such renderings may have been, the sense of dimension or texture achieved with a laser cutter is, of course, a more authentic representation. Laser cutting has also given models a new durability. Whereas previously many small individual units might be shaped and glued together to form a whole part, the precision cutting of the laser has enabled single-piece construction of intricate parts.

As models play an increasingly important role in the design and planning of our environments, the technology of their materials and construction continues to develop. But while synthetic materials and power tools may have expanded the capabilities of the model maker, they have not altogether replaced the exacting handwork practiced by the traditional model maker. Writing about model making in a 1988 issue of *American Craft* magazine, Jeremy Lebensohn noted that "full acceptance of the laser cutter in model making will probably not take place as long as there are shops staffed by experienced craftsmen, with an intuitive knowledge of their work, and master model makers who can organize the thousands of separate jobs required in a complex model." The craft of contemporary model making, then, perhaps remains a collaboration between the knowledgeable appreciation of modern materials and technology and the exacting eye and precise handwork of the traditional craftsperson.

Shearson Lehman Hutton Plaza,
New York, New York
Architect: Kohn Pedersen Fox
Associates PC
Model builder: 3-D Design
Materials: Wood and blueprints
Photographer: © Jack
Pottle/ESTO

Goldman Sachs U.K.
Headquarters, London, England
Architect: Kohn Pedersen Fox
Associates PC
Model builder: Awad Architectural
Models
Materials: Plexiglas and vinyl

RIGHT
Tabor Center, Denver, Colorado
Architect: Kohn Pedersen Fox
Associates PC
Model builder: Awad Architectural
Models
Materials: Plexiglas and vinyl

OPPOSITE AND LEFT
Commonwealth Center, Boston,
Massachusetts
Architect: Kohn Pedersen Fox
Associates PC
Model builder: 3-D Design
Materials: Wood and blueprints
Photographer: © Jock
Pottle/ESTO
Original (left) and updated
versions.

TOP
75 Federal Street, Boston,
Massachusetts
Architect: Kohn Pedersen Fox
Associates PC
Model builder: Awad Architectural
Models
Materials: Plexiglas and vinyl

Harborside Financial Center,
Jersey City, New Jersey
Architect: Beyer Blinder Belle
Model builder: 3-D Design
Materials: Paper

TOP LEFT

Lighthouse model

Architect: Helpern Architects

Model builder: 3-D Design

Materials: Walnut, basswood, cherry

Photographer: © Brian Rose

TOP RIGHT

Bond Building, Sydney, Australia

Architect: Kohn Pedersen Fox Associates PC

Model builder: 3-D Design

Materials: Wood and blueprints

Photographer: © Jock Pottle/ESTO

RIGHT

Addition to the Reed Library, State University College at Fredonia, New York

Architect: Pasanella + Klein, Architects

Model builder: Robert Langelius, Jr.

Materials: Museum board, Plexiglas, aluminum, styrene, and concrete

Photographer: © Jock Pottle/ESTO

MTA West Side Yard
Development, New York,
New York
Architect: Beyer Blinder Belle
Model builder: 3-D Design
Materials: Cherry and basswood
Photographer: © Roy J. Wright

Private residence

Architect: Kupiec & Koutsomitis

Model builder: Lee Trench

Materials: Painted basswood with Plexiglas

Photographer: © Jock Pottle/ESTO

INSIDE THE
MINIATURE

nterior models can serve a wide variety of purposes that more specifically reflect the functions of different interior spaces. These range from the aims of theater set designers, who use models to determine the lighting, color, and placement of flats, to those of clinical psychologists, who use models of the family home to analyze their patients' interactions there. Historians too have made scholarly use of the miniature to investigate the aesthetic and cultural traditions of the past. Among the most resplendent examples of such period rooms are the Thorne Miniature Rooms at the Art Institute of Chicago, stunning nutshells of architecture, interior design, and the decorative arts, ranging over four centuries from the late Tudor to the Modern period. Conceived of and planned by Mrs. James Ward Thorne during the thirties and forties, the period rooms have been constructed on a scale of one inch to one foot and constitute a visual encyclopedia of American and European design history.

Their intricate detailing includes precision plaster work and a clock that actually keeps time. And lest their display appear contrived to excess, Mrs. Thorne also thought to establish a human persona in each room through such devices as an open book or a ball of yarn. While it is their miniature perfection that makes these tableaus intriguing, it is their scale that makes them more practical, and in the end more instructive, period rooms than the full-size model rooms customarily found in museums: a total of sixty-eight period rooms have been assembled and arranged chronologically in a single gallery of the museum.

For the most part, however, the construction of model interiors has less to do with investigating decorative traditions of the past than it does with serving more immediate needs. And unlike such period rooms, most interior models are less preoccupied with the exquisite details of furnishings and decoration. Serving architects and designers rather than historians of the decorative arts, interior models represent the spatial characteristics inside the building—most important, the relationship of the ceiling height to other interior dimensions—and the volume, rather than detail, of interior furnishings and equipment. Such models can be built solely as interior models, or

75 State Street, Boston, Massachusetts
Architect: Graham Gund Architects with Adrian Smith, Skidmore, Owings & Merrill, Chicago
Model builder: Scale Models Unlimited
Photographer: © Steve Rosenthal

they can be assembled inside the larger exterior models, which can then be separated horizontally or vertically to expose an interior view.

As a tool for space planning, interior models serve more specific functions as well, and perhaps the most important of these is their capacity to identify and analyze light sources—natural, incandescent, fluorescent—and their effects on the interior as they vary at different times throughout the day, season, and year. If it is the physical relationships of floor, walls, and ceiling that actually define the volume of an interior, it is the less tangible quality of light that most affects our perception of it. Particularly in the development and design of atrium buildings which proliferate in urban areas, it is this interplay of different light sources that will significantly affect the use and appreciation of the building. Interior models can provide a way of observing those qualities of light—often through tricky maneuvers, as the model will often have one wall open to expose the interior to view.

Interior models are also instrumental in the design of public arenas such as stadiums, concert halls, theaters, and churches, in which architects and designers must investigate the relationship of the different volumes of space meant to serve different private and public functions. Likewise, in such public spaces, models may be a way of determining traffic flow and circulation patterns—not simply issues of design and style, but of public safety as well.

I. M. Pei's Meyerson Symphony Center in Dallas was articulated before construction in a series of interior and exterior models, both for study and presentation. The interior study models investigate the proportions of the interior space, traffic and circulation patterns, and the balance of public and private space. An interior presentation model was also constructed, primarily as a fund-raising tool to present to the client and primary donors to the symphony. Illuminated by fiber optics and wired for sound, the model includes in minute detail the movable acoustical center ceiling panel; its brass, travertine, terrazzo, brushed limestone, and backlit onyx surface finishes; and even the orchestra poised for performance.

While these models seem to have examined every facet of the symphony hall short of its acoustics, some interior models do test acoustics. Such models do not necessarily bear any physical resemblance to the proposed interior; rather, they try to re-create the movement of sound waves, often by reducing the scale of the sound waves to conform to the scale of the model.

Interior models are also instrumental in determining the placement of furniture or equipment. While this may simply be a point of convenience in the model for a residential unit, it may be more critical in the planning of factories and industrial plants where the proximity of different pieces of machinery can involve questions of worker safety. In the layout of office plans, particularly open office plans, models can test different arrangements of work space, equipment, and traffic flow.

Finally, interior models increasingly are proving to be invaluable not only in the design and planning of condominium units, but in their sales and marketing as well. Particularly for those development projects that depend on a percentage of sales before construction, models can familiarize potential buyers with the range of floor plans, sizes, and layouts available. Frequently, if a single floor of a corporate office building can be advanced even by a month, that revenue in turn pays for the model.

Attic, The New York Times Building, New York, New York (photographed inside the unrenovated attic)
Architect: Skidmore, Owings & Merrill
Model builder: Skidmore, Owings & Merrill Model Shop
Photographer: © Peter Aaron/ESTO

Umm al-Qura University, Makkah
al-Mukarramah, Saudi Arabia
Design team: IDEA/Perkins
& Will
Model builder: Scale Models
Unlimited
Photographer: © Steinkamp/
Ballogg, Chicago

75 State Street, Boston,
Massachusetts
Architect: Graham Gund
Architects with Adrian Smith,
Skidmore, Owings & Merrill,
Chicago
Model builder: Scale Models
Unlimited
Photographer: © Steve
Rosenthal

OPPOSITE
125 High Street, Boston,
Massachusetts
Architect: Jung Brannan
Associates
Model builder: Scale Models
Unlimited
Photographer: © Steve
Rosenthal

TOP
Consolidated terminal,
John F. Kennedy Airport,
New York, New York
Architect: Murphy/Jahn
Architects
Model builder: Murphy/Jahn
Architects, PC
Photographer: © Steinkamp/
Ballogg, Chicago

LEFT
New International Terminal,
O'Hare International Airport,
Chicago, Illinois
Design team: Perkins & Will;
Heard & Associates, Ltd;
Consoer, Townsend &
Associates, Inc.
Model builder: Perkins & Will
Photographer: © Steinkamp/
Ballogg, Chicago

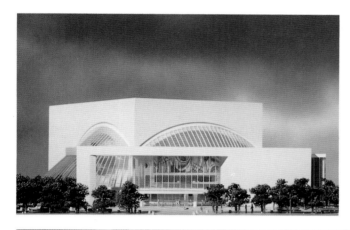

Morton H. Meyerson Symphony
Center, Dallas, Texas
Architect: I. M. Pei & Partners
Model builder: I. M. Pei &
Partners
Photographer: © Nathaniel
Lieberman

181 West Madison,
Chicago, Illinois
Architect: Cesar Pelli &
Associates Inc.
Model builder: Awad Architectural
Models
Photographer: © Bob Shimer,
Hedrich-Blessing

THE ILLUMINATED
MINIATURE

Architectural models can be precise studies of the physical form a building will take; they may examine the engineering feats or the structural underpinnings required to achieve particular dimensions and forms. And they may reproduce facades with highly complex details and ornamentation and explore their fit into the landscape. Often, however, models are less adept at capturing the more atmospheric qualities of a building. By its very nature, the scale of the miniature may prevent it from conveying how one feels standing in the center of an expansive auditorium or beneath the entry to an atrium. While a model can certainly trigger the imagination and memory of such sensations, it cannot fully communicate the more sensory impressions that architecture can evoke.

This said, it follows that lighting is the one tool available to model makers that *can* suggest these more atmospheric qualities of architecture. How we experience architecture has as much to do with the source and type of illumination as with the dimensions of a space, its textures and colors. The combinations of natural and artificial lighting and how these shift throughout the day and evening hours and over the seasons invariably alter our sense of comfort in a space and ultimately our use of it. Recent advances in lighting technology have enabled contemporary models to investigate these less tangible qualities of architecture.

Model illumination meant to convey the actual lighting of the architecture can be reproduced through a variety of means. Often miniature incandescent bulbs such as those used on Christmas trees can be installed in the model to produce intense pinpoints of light.

But if there is to be a multitude of incandescent lights, such an effect might be reproduced better with a single fluorescent tube installed behind ceiling or wall panels that have then been incised at the appropriate points. Or a single fluorescent tube screwed into the base of the model of a skyscraper with many windows can illuminate the entire structure. The use of a fluorescent tube in such an instance would eliminate the need to install many small incandescent bulbs, an impractical, if not impossible, task. Too, it might better simulate the quality of light in many corporate interiors. Similarly, cool neon tubes can be used to produce brighter, more theatrical effects. Both fluorescent and neon tubing generate less heat than incandescent bulbs and thus pose less of a flammability risk. For any interior lighting system, however, a timer can be wired into the circuit to periodically switch off the lighting and cool the system.

Fiber optics, in which filaments of plastic transmit light, are another relatively cool, efficient means of illuminating models. Such a system requires less wiring; moreover, the plastic strands are flexible and can be bent or wound around complex shapes. But the illumination from fiber optics tends to be softer and more diffused because it is transmitted from a single light source; for that reason many model makers prefer to use fiber optics for exterior landscape illumination. And because fiber optics is controlled with a single switch, incandescent illumination—lights connected to a number of different switches and rheostats— may be more flexible.

Not surprisingly, in model building as in the real thing, it is often a combination of different light sources that illuminates the interior most successfully. In the model built for Boston's 75 State Street building (see pages 70 and 75), the interior is illuminated by a combination of 315 miniature incandescent bulbs (in wall sconces and freestanding lighting units) and miniature fluorescent bulbs (for the overhead lighting of office interiors). And in the model built for Chicago Place, incandescent spotlights have been used in conjunction with fluorescent bulbs for storefronts and fiber optics for rows of small interior lights.

Models can be illuminated not simply to reproduce the actual lighting of the proposed building but to emphasize the structure's dramatic effect. Particularly when the model is to be photographed, theatrical lighting can be used to highlight unusual entryways or fenestration, such as that used for the model of the 580 California Street building in San Francisco.

Lighting can also be used to illustrate the effect of the building after sundown. The impact that a new building may have on its environment does not necessarily fade with the daylight, and in urban areas especially, contemporary architecture is often at its most dramatic at night. The illuminated model, of course, best suggests what these effects will be. The models constructed by Benjamin Thompson and Associates for Harborplace and Miami Bayside, both outdoor retail urban marketplaces, were illuminated by miniature incandescent bulbs obtained from a model railroad-supply outlet. When photographed at "dusk," the glittering pinpoints of light create a sparkling, festive atmosphere.

Similarly, part of the dramatic appeal of Los Angeles's Pershing Square is its evening illumination. The grid of the urban park is meant to reflect the the ethnic landscape of the city: Chicano east, African-American southwest, Oriental midtown, and Caucasian west. The design specified that lighting be embedded in the paving surface of the park, making the grid all the more theatrical after sundown. The model of Pershing Square translates the sense of theater through the use of a Plexiglas grid illuminated from below by miniature incandescent bulbs.

Finally, lighting systems can be installed in models to convey information. A computer-controlled LED (light-emitting diode) system on a model intended to promote sales of condominium units can be used, for example, to indicate units that have been sold or units in different price ranges.

Harborplace, Baltimore,
Maryland
Architect: Benjamin Thompson
and Associates
Model builder: Benjamin
Thompson and Associates
Photographer: © Steve
Rosenthal

Holocaust Memorial Museum,
Washington, D.C.
Architect: I. M. Pei & Partners
Model builder: I. M. Pei &
Partners
Photographer: Eric Schiller

8 4

580 California Street, San Francisco, California
Architect: John Burgee Architects; formerly Johnson/Burgee Architects
Model builder: Ron Marian, Joe Chun, Rob Berryman
Photographer: © Bob Harr, Hedrich-Blessing

INNOVA, Houston, Texas

Architect: Cambridge Seven
Associates Inc.

Model builder: F. W. Dixon
Company

Photographer: © Steve
Rosenthal

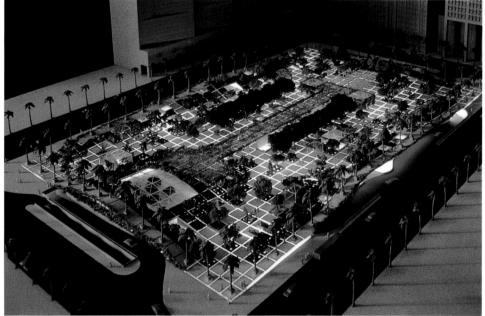

Pershing Square, Los Angeles,
California, shown unilluminated
and illuminated
Architect: SITE, with Kober
Cedergreen Rippon
Model builder: Stomu
Miyazaki/SITE Projects, Inc.

Miami Bayside, Miami, Florida
Architect: Benjamin Thompson
and Associates
Model builder: Benjamin
Thompson and Associates
Photographer: © Steve
Rosenthal

Chicago Place, Chicago, Illinois
Architect: Skidmore, Owings & Merrill
Developer: BCE Development Properties, Inc.
Model builder: Scale Models Unlimited
Photographer: Bob Shimer, Hedrich-Blessing

Linden Court, Hartford,
Connecticut
Architect: Fletcher Thompson
Architects, Engineers, and
Interior Designers
Model builder: Robert M. Hurwit
& Associates
Photographer: © Jock
Pottle/ESTO

THE LANDSCAPE
OF THE MODEL

Model making is not necessarily limited to the construction of a single building. Frequently the proposed building's immediate landscape, urban or rural, is represented as well. Such landscapes serve a variety of purposes. A context model, representing the proposed building in its surrounding environment. is often assembled for an urban building when the scale of new construction is called into question. In such landscapes a finished model of the proposed building is often surrounded by less detailed models of the existing architecture, the latter usually finished in a matte gray. While valuable for demonstrating the schematic massing of buildings or for illustrating the scale of the proposed building in relation to its surroundings, such models can be misleading. With such an obvious focus on one particular structure, they downplay the visual controversies such a building may introduce into the existing environment.

Context models can also represent the proposed building in the same uniform finish as the buildings surrounding it. A case in point is a model of the proposed addition to Frank Lloyd Wright's Guggenheim Museum in New York City. While surely showing the scale of the proposed addition, indeed the fit of the "new" museum into the existing neighborhood, the sense of continuity may be deceptive: the uniformity of the model diminishes the effect of the changes to the existing building and thereby may put into question the conflict the building proposal engendered.

The model for an addition to another museum raises a different point. I. M. Pei's controversial plan for a glass pyramid to be installed within a courtyard of the Louvre was presented in a meticulous model not only of the proposed glass pyramid, but of the Louvre itself. While the design proposal generated international public outcry, the later construction of the pyramid was greeted with more enthusiasm by critics and public alike. The incident raises the question of how much, if indeed at all, a model can evoke the more subtle, atmospheric qualities of architecture and its environment.

Context models can also test the orientation of the proposed building. The 160-foot angled crown of the Citicorp building in New York City was originally designed to face west. A subsequent design, centered around the proposed installation of solar collectors connected to the building's hot water system in the slanted roofline, shifted the slant to face south. When later cost estimates indicated that solar energy could supply only 40 percent of the heating, the plan was scrapped. The slant of the roof is south-facing, however, and only the model remains to represent the building as it was originally designed, facing west.

Proposals for rural buildings reside in an altogether different landscape, both literally and figuratively. For the obvious reason that more space is usually involved, such projects often demand equally expansive models delineating the local topography. The landscape of the model represents not the existing environment, but a design element in itself. And if the landscape is to accommodate a hotel, parking lot, conference center, golf course, and pond, the project will likewise demand that many more building approvals. In many cases too, the topographical model is used for the study of future growth within the community. A model for a condominium proposal, for example, would better serve its purpose with a detailed topographical landscape illustrating the locations of second- and third-stage building. And if traffic patterns and access are to be issues, a precise topographical model will aid in determining sight lines and sign locations.

Moreover, office parks and corporate headquarters in suburban areas are built with the increasing recognition that environmental awareness boosts public image. Consequently a greater percentage of their construction budget is relegated to landscaping. A soothing, naturalistic environment with walkways and shady trees also can make the corporate atmosphere more hospitable and may work to alleviate the stresses associated with the work carried out indoors; an accommodating landscape is viewed as an employee perk that pays its own way. For all of these reasons, it is not unusual now to find landscape architects—whether they work in hard elements such as gravel, asphalt, street furniture, and signage or organic elements including ground cover, trees, shrubs, and flowers—working in a partnership with the building's architects, rather than being called in after construction, as they were often in the past. The models, of course, attest to this new recognition of the importance of the landscape— trees and shrubs can be represented precisely, not simply in terms of shape and size but with exact leaf patterns and true colors.

Landscape architecture is, among other things, the study of where and how the building meets the ground, and models are increasingly used to investigate this intersection. Most significant, models of the landscape are devices that permit the designer to view his or her design at eye level. The firm of Peter Walker and Martha Schwartz uses study models to develop the elements of their landscape; they then photograph the model, often at eye level, as a means of "entering" the space. Such photographs, especially when assembled into a series, can provide a narrative for the landscape and can work as both a design and a presentation tool. A study model for Marina Linear Park in San Diego, California, is a case in point. The landscape architects chose to work with two central images—the linear dimensions of the railroad yards and the grid of the city. To integrate these images in their design of the landscape, the architects planned the park as a vibrant series of bands—of grass, trees, flowers, asphalt, and gravel. The photographs of the model then work to suggest a sense of continuity that the model itself might have more difficulty in achieving.

The irony, of course, is that this sense of space is achieved when the three-dimensional model is translated into the two-dimensional photograph. While the model itself has definite boundaries, the frame of the photograph, especially the close-up photograph of a detail, can suggest a larger sense of space that lies beyond the frame. Using photographs of models in such a way can indeed be a way of investigating the landscape of the proposed building.

The construction of the model landscape serves a purpose beyond simply representing a proposed design. Rolf Janke noted in his comprehensive *Architectural Models*: "Particularly important in building models is human scale. The size of our body is the unit of measurement which we unconsciously apply to the calculation of spatial dimensions. All objects exposed to our view change their emotional effect upon us when they become bigger or smaller than normal. If an architectural model has no accessories to provide scale, it seems to shrink to Lilliputian proportions, when judged with an adult's eyes. A building model, as the reduced version of reality, must have its appropriate scale." So above all, perhaps, a landscape complete with trees, shrubs, waterways, and the appropriately placed pedestrian may endow the model not only with a sense of scale, but with an almost Edenlike sense of harmony, thus generating the goodwill and approval of the public.

There are several ways to represent the contours of the landscape, the simplest being to laminate sheets of cardboard, wood, or cork to represent increments of grade elevations. A more continuous—and more realistic—representation can be achieved with the use of a router adapted to the model maker's particular needs: turned on end and used along with a topographical map, the tool carves polyurethane or polystyrene foam bases to represent the contours of the landscape indicated by the map.

Not surprising in view of its name, the New York City-based architectural firm of SITE is known for its buildings that are frequently observations about architecture and environment, buildings and their sites. The firm's models, then, must convey this consideration of location, topography, geography. Consider the Ansel Adams Center in Carmel, California, that has been designed to appear as though "an incision had been made in the surface of a meadow and a massive plane of grass field tilted upward to form an inclined roof, or 'landscape as building.' " Or the infamous parking-lot showroom, in which asphalt pavement flows over the showroom in a reversal of the customary building and location relationship.

What is particularly revealing and astute about these models is that they investigate the sense of time that invariably affects buildings and their landscapes. As much as we may like to think otherwise, buildings and their environments are not static elements. Over time, buildings change, weather, fade; meadows become forests, shrubs become trees. These are the banal and obvious facts that most models, nevertheless, by nature have difficulty expressing. The SITE models accept, indeed explore, these inevitable occurrences and for that reason are maquettes with an entirely different dimension, prototypes for time as well as for buildings and their landscapes. And in doing so, in spite of all their witticisms, these models demonstrate more wholly the inevitable and continuous relationships that buildings will develop with the natural landscape.

Proposed addition to Solomon R.
Guggenheim Museum,
New York, New York
Architect: Gwathmey Siegel &
Associates
Model builder: Scale Images, Inc.
Photographer: © Dan
Cornish/ESTO

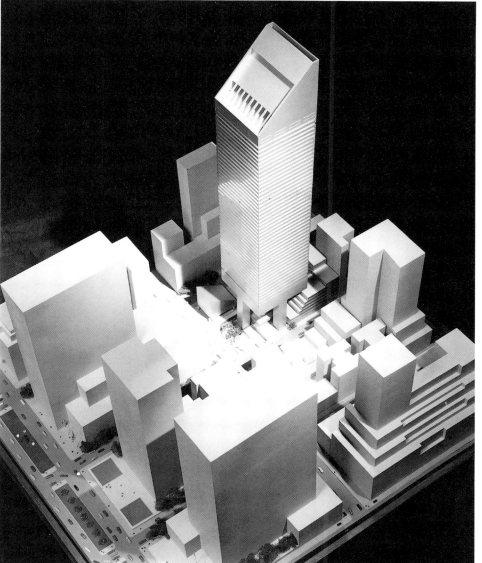

Citicorp Center, New York, New York. The model shows the original, west-facing plan; the photograph of the actual building in place (above) shows the final, southward orientation.
Architect: The Stubbins Associates, Inc.
Model builder: Wally Palladino, Architectural Model Associates
Photographer: Ezra Stoller © ESTO

ABOVE

Linden Court, Hartford,
Connecticut
Architect: Fletcher Thompson
Architects, Engineers, and
Interior Designers
Model builder: Robert M. Hurwit
& Associates
Photographer: © Jock
Pottle/ESTO

RIGHT

Addition to Le Grand Louvre,
Paris, France
Architect: I. M. Pei & Partners
Model builder: Resine Sorl
Photographer: Dahliette
Sucheyre

Marina Linear Park,
San Diego, California
Landscape architect: The Office
of Peter Walker and Martha
Schwartz
Model builder: The Office of
Peter Walker and Martha
Schwartz
Photographer: David Walker

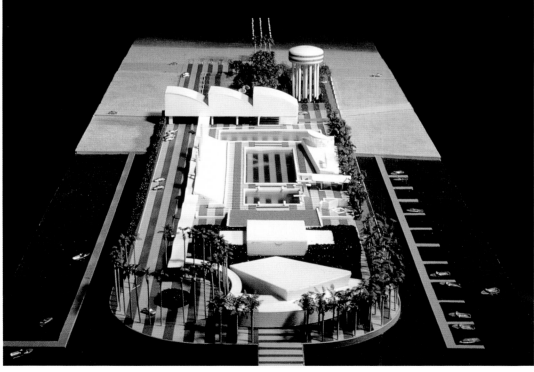

International Swimming Hall of
Fame, Fort Lauderdale, Florida
Architect: Arquitectonica
Landscape architect: The Office
of Peter Walker and Martha
Schwartz
Model builder: The Office of
Peter Walker and Martha
Schwartz
Photographer: David Walker

TOP
Proposed parking-lot showroom,
site undetermined
Architect: SITE Projects, Inc.
Model builder: James Wines

RIGHT
Proposed The Friends of
Photography—Ansel Adams
Center, Carmel, California
Architect: SITE Projects, Inc.
Model builder: James Wines

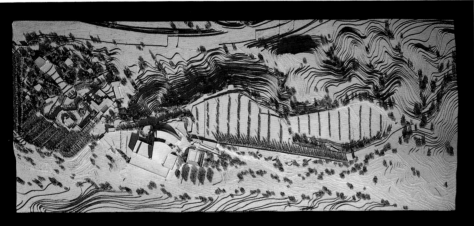

ABOVE

Proposed Cornell University
Alumni and Development Center,
Ithaca, New York
Architect: Richard Meier &
Partners Architects
Model builder: Richard Meier &
Partners Architects
Photographer: Ezra Stoller ©
ESTO

LEFT

Santa Fe Opera, Santa Fe,
New Mexico
Architect: James Stewart Polshek
and Partners
Design team: D. B. Middleton,
senior designer; Tyler Huntington
Donaldson, design associate;
Sara Elizabeth Caples,
management associate; Mary
Beth Comins, design team.
Model builder: Mary Beth Comins
Photographer: © Dan
Cornish/ESTO

First Interstate Bank at Fountain
Place, Dallas, Texas
Architect: I. M. Pei & Partners
Model builder: George Gabriel, I.
M. Pei & Partners
Photographer: Bob Harr,
Hedrich-Blessing

MODEL BUILDING
AND PHOTOGRAPHY

I n recent years the photograph of the model has evolved into a separate art form. Model photography first grew in demand during the immediate postwar years, when building construction was limited because of the shortage of materials. The editors of architecture and design magazines, realizing that their readers were anxious to see the architecture emerging from war research, materials, and technology, satisfied them by publishing the models of these buildings—often photographed in such lifelike ways that it was difficult to determine these were only models. It took architects and designers little time to realize that the photograph of the model could be a valuable resource itself, a way to position the building on its site and to examine its fit into the existing environment.

Contemporary model photography continues to serve that purpose. In addition, because models are fragile and transporting them can be impractical, a photograph of the model may be the most practical way to show the design of a proposed building to a large number of developers, contractors, tenants, design partners, and other interested parties. Most significant, perhaps, are those photographs used to market a building to proposed tenants, and in such cases, photographs of the model can boost sales. Model photography, particularly that which idealizes or glamorizes the proposed building, is a graphic device especially valuable to developers who are trying to create an appealing leasing package before the building has been constructed.

But if architectural photography is a means of witnessing architecture secondhand, the photograph of the model is a sort of thirdhand representation of the building. Often it is an unwitting collaboration between model maker, architect, and photographer, and what we see in the photograph is an image constructed deliberately through stages to create a specific impression. Consider a photograph taken from the base of the model for the Citicorp building built in New York City in 1978. The photograph emphasizes the proposed tower's massive base looming over dwarfed pedestrians and automobiles. While such a photograph may have created a powerful and positive image in the mid-seventies when urban architecture engendered a more imposing presence, it might be a less persuasive selling tool in today's market, when critics and public alike have raised a clamor for a more human, and less threatening, scale in their urban landscape.

It is not simply the images that have changed in the photography of models. Montage photography, in which a photograph of the model is delicately inserted into a photograph of the existing streetscape, has achieved a new level of sophistication that is not wasted on architects, developers, urban planners—indeed anyone with an interest in viewing slices of a future urban landscape. While the presentation model may be a first step toward this view, to position it in the existing environment before construction starts is a more recent and persuasive visual aid for envisioning the fit of a building into its landscape. While a context model may be a three-dimensional means of doing the same thing, a composite photograph may often be the more realistic representation.

The electronic age has yielded a new sophistication in such composite photography. Whereas in earlier days it might be achieved with a razor, a steady hand, and a tube of glue, contemporary photo montages, achieved with emulsion stripping and computer retouching, create more persuasive, albeit illusory, results. Pioneered by the Chicago-based architectural photography firm of Hedrich-Blessing, such photography demands first an acute visual analysis of the site of the proposed building—the angles from which it might best be viewed and its light at different hours of the day. The site is then photographed. These angles and lighting conditions must then be reconstructed in the studio where the model is photographed. The image of the model must be scaled to correspond with the scale of the existing buildings. Both images are then submitted to the emulsion stripper, who lifts the emulsions from the base of both transparencies and then combines fragments of each to create a new single image. To achieve an even more faultless image, the film can then be submitted for computer retouching, which can perfect color, lighting, shading, and the blending of images.

While it is the purpose of most montage photography to install the proposed building into the existing landscape unobtrusively, some montage photography intends from the start to be more dramatic. The proposed building, after all, is not meant to be indistinguishable. The use of filters, then, can highlight or delineate the profile of the building. By splicing together the high-contrast photograph of the proposed building with a low-contrast photograph of the landscape, the building will, of course, be more noticeable.

While all of these photographic procedures can add substantial costs to the already high price of the model, if it works to boost the occupancy rate of the proposed building before it is open for business, the photograph more than repays the cost.

The applications for composite photography for marketing architecture are obvious, and with the increasing sophistication of the technology comes increased use. And there the ethical questions are raised. Such composites of the real and unreal, built and unbuilt worlds, raise questions not simply about the accuracy in such documentation, but about its honesty. The miniature landscape, by its very nature, offers the viewer more sight lines than the actual building ever will. The model can be seen from levels beneath its base or far above it, not to mention the infinity of angles at its own level. While a sequence of such photographs may narrate the architecture in a logical, composed sequence, such a narrative is impossible to translate in the real, built world; and in a way, then, it may be ultimately irrelevant. The angles from which we will actually see most buildings are, of course, far more limited.

It is in the nature of model photography to capitalize on the availability of these sight lines, and the angle of the camera can manipulate the final image to any number of desired effects. Originally, such photographs were assembled to help the architect visualize more completely the relationship between the building and the existing environment. They were an attempt to create a more holistic vision of the proposed building, a way to frame it within its landscape and lighting, and a way to give the model even greater authenticity. But the increased use of models for marketing architecture raises new questions. If the site of the proposed building is in a historic district, for example, a photograph in which the visual impact of any new construction is minimized might encourage community approval. Or if the height of the building is controversial, to be of much benefit to its developers, the photograph submitted to zoning and community boards might be taken from an angle minimizing its height. Too, such montage photography does not take into account future construction or other changes to the site beyond, of course, the construction of the proposed building.

Montage photographs of the model for the proposed South Ferry Plaza building at the southern tip of New York's Manhattan Island demonstrate how such realistic photographs can nevertheless suggest their own truths. Designed by the architectural firms of Fox & Fowle Associates, PC, and Frank Williams & Associates Architects, the tower is not entirely inconsistent in height with the other buildings in the financial district. Still, the three photographs show how the viewpoint can emphasize or diminish the effect of the new construction on the existing skyline. One distant view across New York Harbor presents the building as akin in height to the soaring towers of the World Trade Center, while another view, somewhat closer, presents it as more consistent in height with its immediate neighbors. A third and almost comic representation captures only the tip of its dome and spire above the rooftop of an adjacent office building, downplaying its effect altogether.

Finally, and most dramatic, perhaps, are those photographs that represent a view that most street viewers will never experience. A photograph of an early design for New York City's Columbus Center by Moshe Safdie & Associates records the proposed building's dramatic trajectory above an ocean of trees in Central Park. It is a view, however, that might be enjoyed more conveniently by pigeons than by pedestrians. Such composite photography may fascinate and intrigue us into imagining the unbuilt world; for all its technical proficiency, however, its accuracy in doing so should be viewed realistically, with a dose of skepticism.

The obvious fact remains that what we are looking at is not the building but a photograph of the building. In the words of one architectural photographer, "It's not so much a lie, as the absence of truth." As a way of interpreting the future, such photographs are bound, by their very nature, to be subjective more than they are documentary. Inevitably they straddle the line between artifice and authenticity—which, perhaps, is exactly why they seize the imagination with such force.

Lake & Wells Building,
Chicago, Illinois
Architect: Murphy/Jahn
Architects, PC
Model builder: Scale Models
Unlimited
Photographer: Bob Harr, Bob
Shimer, Hedrich-Blessing

OPPOSITE

First Interstate Bank at Fountain
Place, Dallas, Texas
Architect: I. M. Pei & Partners
Model builder: George Gabriel,
I. M. Pei & Partners
Photographer: Bob Harr,
Hedrich-Blessing

LEFT

900 North Michigan,
Chicago, Illinois
Architect: Kohn Pedersen Fox
Associates PC
Model builder: Awad Architectural
Models
Photographer: Bob Shimer,
Hedrich-Blessing

ABOVE
Miami Arena, Miami, Florida,
photographed against the actual
ocean
Architect: Alfred Browing Parker,
Architect
Model builder: Miami
Modelbuilders
Photographer: Ezra Stoller ©
ESTO

RIGHT
Citicorp Center, New York,
New York
Architect: The Stubbins
Associates, Inc.
Model builder: Wally Palladino,
Architectural Model Associates
Photographer: Ezra Stoller ©
ESTO

Columbus Center,
New York, New York
Architect: Moshe Safdie &
Associates, Inc.
Model builder: Awad Architectural
Models
Photographer: © Steve
Rosenthal

South Ferry Plaza,
New York, New York
Architect: Fox & Fowle Architects,
PC, and Frank Williams &
Associates Architects
Model builder: Scale Images, Inc.
Photographer: © Dan
Cornish/ESTO

75 State Street, Boston, Massachusetts (in center of photograph)
Architect: Graham Gund Architects with Adrian Smith, Skidmore, Owings & Merrill, Chicago
Model builder: Scale Models Unlimited
Photographer: © Steve Rosenthal

Trump City, New York, New York
Architect: Cooper, Robertson +
Partners
Model builder: Cooper,
Robertson + Partners
Photographer: © Jeff
Goldberg/ESTO

THE UNBUILT
LANDSCAPE

rchitectural models are not limited to conjectures on the physical, built world. They can be small constructions drawn from the psychic universe, visual metaphors that express truths of the soul rather than the more mundane truths of engineering. Such models should not be dismissed as exercises in whimsy. Architecture leaves relatively little room for experimentation. The scale of a building, its cost, and its utility are the obvious factors that prevent it from being a purely ideological or aesthetic polemic. Unlike a canvas hanging on a wall, a sonata, or an epic poem, buildings must nurture the body as well as the soul. For the architect, then, the model is sometimes the place where the vagaries of the human imagination can be most happily assembled.

Such was the case with the series of models for lighthouses, small beacons to be constructed nowhere but in their designers' imaginations. Designed for an auction to benefit New York City's Lighthouse Child Development Center, the series of conceptual pieces investigated the various metaphors represented by the image of a lighthouse: guidance, safety, a source of light, the point of entry, a safe harbor. The criteria stipulated only that the models be less than twenty inches in height, that the diameter not exceed twelve inches, and that the model be illuminated.

Indeed, the diversity and potency of the image were apparent in these small assemblages. The lighthouse submitted by SITE, for example, has a dark side and a light side, "embodying the dichotomy of light and dark, [in which] the traditional lighthouse becomes a literal expression of its function." That submitted by Fox & Fowle Architects, PC investigates the spiraling trajectory of the image, while the lighthouse by Lydia DePolo is a shimmering beacon, standing on a base "that enables building on sand and mud."

The contemporary movement in architecture known as deconstructivism suggests that architecture is not simply the art and industry of building functional shelters. The movement proposes that architecture can also express more intellectual theories of enclosure and openness, structure and space, inside and out. Not surprisingly, architects who work in these metaphors do not necessarily build them. They do construct the models, however, as physical evidence of their speculations. The models constructed by the firm of Ellerbe Becket for an airline terminal and for the school of architecture at the University of Minnesota, for all their sharp angles and amalgam of materials, are the lyrical physical expression of some of these theories.

Architectural competitions are also fertile ground for this landscape of the imagination. For valuable downtown urban plots, developers may have little difficulty in persuading architects to go to the time and expense of submitting complex models for building proposals they may have only a small chance of winning. Such models provide an often fascinating glimpse of the unbuilt city, provoking comparisons between the city that might have been and the city that is. The office towers for the Madison Square Garden site in New York City were designed by Richard Meier & Partners for a development proposal based on the assumption that the existing Madison Square Garden would be relocated. By replacing the sports arena and convention hall with office towers, the developers were also relying on a shift of character and use of a particular city neighborhood. Whether the construction of these towers would reflect the change that had already come about in this particular New York City neighborhood or would itself instigate this change is unclear; as in so much urban development, both statements probably have some degree of truth. Still, such models of the unbuilt city indicate that the urban landscape as it might have been is only as fantastic as the one that is.

Of other projects that simply never get built—for reasons of cost, approvals denied, or any number of other myriad factors that contribute to urban construction—only the models remain to show us the cityscape that might have been. An early study model for Trump City illustrates the sprawling waterfront development project that would, among other things, reestablish New York City's dubious honor of being home to the world's tallest building. Planned for a seventy-six acre site, currently occupied by an abandoned freight yard and piers, the mixed-use development project would also include nineteen acres of parks and promenades, office and residential buildings, as well as retail shops in an expansive plan that would irrevocably redefine the character of Manhattan's Upper West Side.

It is doubtful that Trump City will ever be constructed on the lavish scale of its early proposals. Its model, however, will remain to represent its soaring aspirations. What the models on these pages tell us, then, is that architectural models are not simply patterns for the built landscape. Like the lighthouses, they can work as prototypes for the imaginative process. Or, like those cityscapes that have never been constructed, they can work as miniature dioramas, showing us how we define and plan our cities and, more important, our place in them.

TOP

Consolidated terminal for
American Airlines, Northwest
Airlines, John F. Kennedy
Airport, New York, New York
Architect: Leibowitz/Ellerbe
Becket, New York, and Ellerbe
Becket, Inc., New York office
Model builder: Ellerbe
Becket, Inc.
Photographer: © Dan
Cornish/ESTO

LEFT

University of Minnesota School
of Architecture, Minneapolis,
Minnesota
Architect: Ellerbe Becket, Inc.,
New York and Minneapolis
offices
Photographer: © Dan
Cornish/ESTO

Madison Square Garden Site
Redevelopment Competition,
New York, New York
Architect: Richard Meier &
Partners Architects
Model builder: Awad Architectural
Models
Photographer: Ezra Stoller ©
ESTO

TOP LEFT

Lighthouse model

Architect: Kohn Pedersen Fox

Associates PC

Model builder: Kohn Pedersen

Fox Associates PC

TOP RIGHT

"Pharos" Lighthouse

Architect: Lydia DePolo,

DePolo/Dunbar

Model builder: DePolo/Dunbar

RIGHT

Lighthouse model

Architect: Fox & Fowle

Architects, PC

Model builder: Fox & Fowle

Architects, PC

1 2 2

ABOVE

Lighthouse model
Architect: SITE Projects, Inc.
Model builder: SITE Projects, Inc.

LEFT

Lighthouse model
Architect: Robert A. M. Stern
Architects
Model builder: Eisenhardt Mills

DIRECTORY OF MODEL SHOPS AND STUDIOS

Awad Architectural Models Inc.
260 West 36th Street
New York, NY 10018

F. W. Dixon
55 Salem Street
Wobum, MA 01801

Eisenhardt Mills
1510 Richmond Rd.
Easton, PA 18042

Gabriel Models
14 Boxwood Drive
Fairfield, NJ 07006

Robert M. Hurwit & Associates
18 Pleasant Drive
Cheshire, CT 06410

Maloof Model Makers, Inc.
27 West 24th Street
New York, NY 10010

The Model Shop
345 North Canal
Chicago, IL 60606

Scale Images, Inc.
840 Nepperhan Avenue
Yonkers, NY 10703

Scale Models Unlimited
320 West Ohio Street
Chicago, IL 60610

Scale Models Unlimited
111 Independence Drive
Menlo Park, CA 94025

3-D Design
155 East Lincoln Avenue
Mount Vernon, NY 10522

SELECTED BIBLIOGRAPHY

BOOKS AND EXHIBITION CATALOGS

Cleaver, John. *Constructing Model Buildings*. New York: St. Martin's Press, 1973.

Hendrick, Thomas William. *The Modern Architectural Model*. London: Architectural Press, 1957.

Hohauser, Sanford. *Architecture and Interior Models*. Rev. ed. New York: Van Nostrand Reinhold, 1982.

Janke, Rolf. *Architectural Models*. New York: Architectural Book Publishing Company, 1978.

Miniature Environments. Catalog to the exhibition at the Whitney Museum of American Art at Philip Morris, August 2 to September 27, 1989. With an essay by Josephine Gear.

New New York: Architectural Models from the Last Decade. Catalog to the exhibition at the Queens Museum, July 30 to September 27, 1987. With an essay by Robert A. M. Stern with Thomas Mellins.

Renoir, Tony. *How to Make Architectural Models*. London: Studio Vista, 1973.

Taylor, J. R. *Model Building for Architects and Engineers*. New York: McGraw-Hill, 1971.

Weiss, Harvey. *Model Buildings and How to Make Them*. New York: Crowell, 1979.

ARTICLES

Aldersey-Williams, Hugh. "Perfect Fakes." *Industrial Design*, November – December 1987, 56 – 61.

Aydelott, A. L. "Making a House Model." *Progressive Architecture*, October 1949, 69 – 70.

Backlund, Nick. "Lighthouses." *Industrial Design*, January/February 1989, 68 – 71.

Bazjanac, Vladimir. "Computer Simulation: A Realistic Assessment." *Progressive Architecture*, July 1971, 80 – 82.

Carter, Ann. "Idea as Model Seriously Impractical." *Progressive Architecture*, February 1977, 30 – 31.

"Design Review: Master Models." *Architectural Review*, December 1976, 367 – 68.

Gomez, Edward M. "From Plaything to Hobby." *Metropolis*, July/August 1989.

Herman, Arthur E. "Models of Plastics and Aluminum." *Progressive Architecture*, December 1959, 9 – 11.

"How to Make the Most of Your Models." *Journal of the American Institute of Architects*, April 1967, 84 – 86.

Jacobs, Jane. "The Miniature Boom." *Architectural Forum*, May 1958, 106 – 11.

Lebensohn, Jeremy. "Mighty Miniatures." *American Craft*, June/July 1988.

Oliver, Joe. "Architectural Photocomposition." *Photomethods*, March 1989, 34 – 35.

"Small Town." *The New Yorker*, 8 May 1989, 33 – 34.

INDEX

REFERENCE··NOT TO BE
TAKEN FROM THIS ROOM